SYSTEM 20

A 20 Day Plan To Take Control Of Your Health

This Planner Belongs to :

....

✉ ....   ‖‖‖‖‖ ‖‖‖‖‖‖‖‖‖‖‖‖‖‖
D1715007

@ ....

📞 ....

Table of Contents

Day 1

My System 20 Morning Routine

Date: _____   Calories: _____

Meditation & Stretch

Start time   ....

Duration   ....

Meditation score ....

1	2	3	4	5
V. Poor			V. Good	

Coffee with MCT oil

Start time   ....

Duration   ....

Coffee MCT oil score ....

1	2	3	4	5
V. Poor			V. Good	

Cardio Routine

Start time   ....

Duration   ....

Cardio score   ....

1	2	3	4	5
V. Poor			V. Good	

Notes

....
....
....
....
....
....
....
....
....
....

My System 20 Diet Daily Plan

Date: Calories:

No Breakfast

Skip breakfast

Start eating at 11 a.m

Start eating time ....

Start eating score ....

1	2	3	4	5
V. Poor				V. Good

Lunch

.... tbsp apple cider vinegar

Beans ....

Greens ....

Protiens ....

Lunch score ....

1	2	3	4	5
V. Poor				V. Good

Snacks

Lean deli meat ....

Nuts ....

Guacamole ....

Cottage ....

Cheese ....

Green olives ....

Kale Chips ....

Eggs ....

Cheese Chips ....

Snacks score ....

1	2	3	4	5
V. Poor				V. Good

Dinner

.... tbsp apple cider vinegar

Beans ....

Greens ....

Protiens ....

Dinner score ....

Stop eating at 7 PM

Stop eating score ....

1	2	3	4	5
V. Poor				V. Good

My System 20 Night Routine

Date: _____   Calories: _____

Sleep

Went to bed at ....

Take to fall asleep ....

Get out of bed at ....

Total sleep hours ....

Sleep score ....

1	2	3	4	5
V. Poor			V. Good	

Wake up

Wake up goal at ....

Actual wake up at ....

Wake up score ....

Wake up same
Time score ....

1	2	3	4	5
V. Poor			V. Good	

To do

Turned off tech at ....

Turning off tech score ....

Text conversation with
....

No caffeine at ....

No caffeine score ....

1	2	3	4	5
V. Poor			V. Good	

Notes

....
....
....
....
....
....
....
....
....
....
....

My System 20 Recipe

Prep Time : | Cook Time : | Serves :

Name : ....

Ingredients

....

....

....

....

....

....

....

....

....

....

Directions :

....

....

....

....

....

....

....

....

My System 20 Recipe

Prep Time : | Cook Time : | Serves :

Name : ....

Ingredients

....
....
....
....
....
....
....
....
....
....

Directions :

....
....
....
....
....
....
....
....
....

My System 20 Recipe

Prep Time : | Cook Time : | Serves :

Name : ....

Ingredients

....
....
....
....
....
....
....
....
....
....
....

Directions :

....
....
....
....
....
....
....
....
....

Day 2

My System 20 Morning Routine

Date: _____   Calories: _____

Meditation & Stretch

Start time ....

Duration ....

Meditation score ....

1	2	3	4	5
V. Poor				V. Good

Coffee with MCT oil

Start time ....

Duration ....

Coffee MCT oil score ....

1	2	3	4	5
V. Poor				V. Good

Cardio Routine

Start time ....

Duration ....

Cardio score ....

1	2	3	4	5
V. Poor				V. Good

Notes

....
....
....
....
....
....
....
....
....
....

My System 20 Diet Daily Plan

Date: Calories:

No Breakfast

Skip breakfast

Start eating at 11 a.m

Start eating time   ....

Start eating score   ....

1	2	3	4	5
V. Poor			V. Good	

Lunch

.... tbsp apple cider vinegar

Beans   ....

Greens   ....

Protiens   ....

Lunch score   ....

1	2	3	4	5
V. Poor			V. Good	

Snacks

Lean deli meat	....
Nuts	....
Guacamole	....
Cottage	....
Cheese	....
Green olives	....
Kale Chips	....
Eggs	....
Cheese Chips	....
Snacks score	....

1	2	3	4	5
V. Poor			V. Good	

Dinner

.... tbsp apple cider vinegar

Beans   ....

Greens   ....

Protiens   ....

Dinner score   ....

Stop eating at 7 PM

Stop eating score ....

1	2	3	4	5
V. Poor			V. Good	

My System 20 Night Routine

Date: ....   Calories: ....

Sleep

Went to bed at ....

Take to fall asleep ....

Get out of bed at ....

Total sleep hours ....

Sleep score ....

1	2	3	4	5
V. Poor				V. Good

Wake up

Wake up goal at ....

Actual wake up at ....

Wake up score ....

Wake up same
Time score ....

1	2	3	4	5
V. Poor				V. Good

To do

Turned off tech at ....

Turning off tech score ....

Text conversation with

....

No caffeine at ....

No caffeine score ....

1	2	3	4	5
V. Poor				V. Good

Notes

....

....

....

....

....

....

....

....

....

....

My System 20 Recipe

Prep Time : | Cook Time : | Serves :

Name : ....

Ingredients

....

....

....

....

....

....

....

....

....

....

Directions :

....

....

....

....

....

....

....

....

....

My System 20 Recipe

Prep Time : | Cook Time : | Serves :

Name : ....

Ingredients

....

....

....

....

....

....

....

....

....

....

Directions :

....

....

....

....

....

....

....

....

....

....

My System 20 Recipe

Prep Time : | Cook Time : | Serves :

Name : ....

Ingredients

....

....

....

....

....

....

....

....

....

....

Directions :

....

....

....

....

....

....

....

....

....

Day 3

My System 20 Morning Routine

Date: ....   Calories: ....

Meditation & Stretch

Start time   ....

Duration   ....

Meditation score   ....

1   2   3   4   5

V. Poor   V. Good

Coffee with MCT oil

Start time   ....

Duration   ....

Coffee MCT oil score   ....

1   2   3   4   5

V. Poor   V. Good

Cardio Routine

Start time   ....

Duration   ....

Cardio score   ....

1   2   3   4   5

V. Poor   V. Good

Notes

....

....

....

....

....

....

....

....

....

....

....

My System 20 Diet Daily Plan

Date: Calories:

No Breakfast

Skip breakfast

Start eating at 11 a.m

Start eating time ....

Start eating score ....

1	2	3	4	5
V. Poor			V. Good	

Lunch

.... tbsp apple cider vinegar

Beans   ....

Greens   ....

Protiens   ....

Lunch score   ....

1	2	3	4	5
V. Poor			V. Good	

Snacks

Lean deli meat   ....
Nuts   ....
Guacamole   ....
Cottage   ....
Cheese
Green olives   ....
Kale Chips   ....
Eggs   ....
Cheese Chips   ....

Snacks score   ....

1	2	3	4	5
V. Poor			V. Good	

Dinner

.... tbsp apple cider vinegar

Beans   ....

Greens   ....

Protiens   ....

Dinner score   ....

Stop eating at 7 PM

Stop eating score ....

1	2	3	4	5
V. Poor			V. Good	

My System 20 Night Routine

Date: ....   Calories: ....

Sleep

Went to bed at ....

Take to fall asleep ....

Get out of bed at ....

Total sleep hours ....

Sleep score ....

1	2	3	4	5
V. Poor			V. Good	

Wake up

Wake up goal at ....

Actual wake up at ....

Wake up score ....

Wake up same
Time score ....

1	2	3	4	5
V. Poor			V. Good	

To do

Turned off tech at ....

Turning off tech score ....

Text conversation with
....

No caffeine at ....

No caffeine score ....

1	2	3	4	5
V. Poor			V. Good	

Notes

....
....
....
....
....
....
....
....
....

My System 20 Recipe

Prep Time : | Cook Time : | Serves :

Name : ....

Ingredients

Directions :

My System 20 Recipe

Prep Time : | Cook Time : | Serves :

Name : ....

Ingredients

Directions :

My System 20 Recipe

Prep Time : | Cook Time : | Serves :

Name : ....

Ingredients

....
....
....
....
....
....
....
....
....
....
....
....

Directions :

....
....
....
....
....
....
....
....
....

Day 4

My System 20 Morning Routine

Date: Calories:

Meditation & Stretch

Start time   ....

Duration   ....

Meditation score ....

1	2	3	4	5
V. Poor			V. Good	

Coffee with MCT oil

Start time   ....

Duration   ....

Coffee MCT oil score ....

1	2	3	4	5
V. Poor			V. Good	

Cardio Routine

Start time   ....

Duration   ....

Cardio score   ....

1	2	3	4	5
V. Poor			V. Good	

Notes

....

....

....

....

....

....

....

....

....

....

....

My System 20 Diet Daily Plan

Date: Calories:

No Breakfast

Skip breakfast

Start eating at 11 a.m

Start eating time ....

Start eating score ....

1	2	3	4	5
V. Poor			V. Good	

Lunch

.... tbsp apple cider vinegar

Beans   ....

Greens   ....

Protiens   ....

Lunch score   ....

1	2	3	4	5
V. Poor			V. Good	

Snacks

Lean deli meat   ....

Nuts   ....

Guacamole   ....

Cottage   ....

Cheese   ....

Green olives   ....

Kale Chips   ....

Eggs   ....

Cheese Chips   ....

Snacks score   ....

1	2	3	4	5
V. Poor			V. Good	

Dinner

.... tbsp apple cider vinegar

Beans   ....

Greens   ....

Protiens   ....

Dinner score   ....

Stop eating at 7 PM

Stop eating score ....

1	2	3	4	5
V. Poor			V. Good	

My System 20 Night Routine

Date: _____   Calories: _____

Sleep

Went to bed at ....

Take to fall asleep ....

Get out of bed at ....

Total sleep hours ....

Sleep score ....

1	2	3	4	5
V. Poor			V. Good	

Wake up

Wake up goal at ....

Actual wake up at ....

Wake up score ....

Wake up same
Time score ....

1	2	3	4	5
V. Poor			V. Good	

To do

Turned off tech at ....

Turning off tech score ....

Text conversation with
....

No caffeine at ....

No caffeine score ....

1	2	3	4	5
V. Poor			V. Good	

Notes

....
....
....
....
....
....
....
....
....
....
....

My System 20 Recipe

Prep Time : | Cook Time : | Serves :

Name : ....

Ingredients

Directions :

My System 20 Recipe

Prep Time : | Cook Time : | Serves :

Name : ....

Ingredients

....

....

....

....

....

....

....

....

....

....

Directions :

....

....

....

....

....

....

....

....

My System 20 Recipe

Prep Time : | Cook Time : | Serves :

Name : ....

Ingredients

Directions :

Day 5

My System 20 Morning Routine

Date: ....   Calories: ....

Meditation & Stretch

Start time ....

Duration ....

Meditation score ....

1	2	3	4	5
V. Poor			V. Good	

Coffee with MCT oil

Start time ....

Duration ....

Coffee MCT oil score ....

1	2	3	4	5
V. Poor			V. Good	

Cardio Routine

Start time ....

Duration ....

Cardio score ....

1	2	3	4	5
V. Poor			V. Good	

Notes

....
....
....
....
....
....
....
....
....
....

My System 20 Diet Daily Plan

Date: Calories:

No Breakfast

Skip breakfast

Start eating at 11 a.m

Start eating time ....

Start eating score ....

1	2	3	4	5
V. Poor			V. Good	

Lunch

.... tbsp apple cider vinegar

Beans   ....

Greens   ....

Protiens   ....

Lunch score   ....

1	2	3	4	5
V. Poor			V. Good	

Snacks

Lean deli meat   ....

Nuts   ....

Guacamole   ....

Cottage   ....

Cheese   ....

Green olives   ....

Kale Chips   ....

Eggs   ....

Cheese Chips   ....

Snacks score   ....

1	2	3	4	5
V. Poor			V. Good	

Dinner

.... tbsp apple cider vinegar

Beans   ....

Greens   ....

Protiens   ....

Dinner score   ....

Stop eating at 7 PM

Stop eating score   ....

1	2	3	4	5
V. Poor			V. Good	

My System 20 Night Routine

Date: ....   Calories: ....

Sleep

Went to bed at ....

Take to fall asleep ....

Get out of bed at ....

Total sleep hours ....

Sleep score ....

1	2	3	4	5
V. Poor			V. Good	

Wake up

Wake up goal at ....

Actual wake up at ....

Wake up score ....

Wake up same
Time score ....

1	2	3	4	5
V. Poor			V. Good	

To do

Turned off tech at ....

Turning off tech score ....

Text conversation with
....

No caffeine at ....

No caffeine score ....

1	2	3	4	5
V. Poor			V. Good	

Notes

....
....
....
....
....
....
....
....
....
....

My System 20 Recipe

Prep Time : | Cook Time : | Serves :

Name : ....

Ingredients

....

....

....

....

....

....

....

....

....

....

Directions :

....

....

....

....

....

....

....

....

....

My System 20 Recipe

Prep Time : | Cook Time : | Serves :

Name : ....

Ingredients

....

....

....

....

....

....

....

....

....

....

Directions :

....

....

....

....

....

....

....

....

My System 20 Recipe

Prep Time : | Cook Time : | Serves :

Name : ....

Ingredients

....

....

....

....

....

....

....

....

....

....

Directions :

....

....

....

....

....

....

....

....

Day 6

My System 20 Morning Routine

Date: Calories:

Meditation & Stretch

Start time   ....

Duration   ....

Meditation score ....

1	2	3	4	5
V. Poor			V. Good	

Coffee with MCT oil

Start time   ....

Duration   ....

Coffee MCT oil score ....

1	2	3	4	5
V. Poor			V. Good	

Cardio Routine

Start time   ....

Duration   ....

Cardio score   ....

1	2	3	4	5
V. Poor			V. Good	

Notes

....
....
....
....
....
....
....
....
....
....

My System 20 Diet Daily Plan

Date: Calories:

No Breakfast

Skip breakfast

Start eating at 11 a.m

Start eating time ....

Start eating score ....

1	2	3	4	5
V. Poor			V. Good	

Lunch

.... tbsp apple cider vinegar

Beans   ....

Greens   ....

Protiens   ....

Lunch score   ....

1	2	3	4	5
V. Poor			V. Good	

Snacks

Lean deli meat	....
Nuts	....
Guacamole	....
Cottage	....
Cheese	....
Green olives	....
Kale Chips	....
Eggs	....
Cheese Chips	....
Snacks score	....

1	2	3	4	5
V. Poor			V. Good	

Dinner

.... tbsp apple cider vinegar

Beans   ....

Greens   ....

Protiens   ....

Dinner score   ....

Stop eating at 7 PM

Stop eating score ....

1	2	3	4	5
V. Poor			V. Good	

My System 20 Night Routine

Date: _____   Calories: _____

Sleep

Went to bed at ....

Take to fall asleep ....

Get out of bed at ....

Total sleep hours ....

Sleep score ....

1	2	3	4	5
V. Poor			V. Good	

Wake up

Wake up goal at ....

Actual wake up at ....

Wake up score ....

Wake up same
Time score ....

1	2	3	4	5
V. Poor			V. Good	

To do

Turned off tech at ....

Turning off tech score ....

Text conversation with
....

No caffeine at ....

No caffeine score ....

1	2	3	4	5
V. Poor			V. Good	

Notes

....
....
....
....
....
....
....
....
....
....
....

My System 20 Recipe

Prep Time : | Cook Time : | Serves :

Name : ....

Ingredients

....
....
....
....
....
....
....
....
....
....
....
....

Directions :

....
....
....
....
....
....
....
....
....

My System 20 Recipe

Prep Time : | Cook Time : | Serves :

Name : ....

Ingredients

....

....

....

....

....

....

....

....

....

....

Directions :

....

....

....

....

....

....

....

....

....

My System 20 Recipe

Prep Time : | Cook Time : | Serves :

Name : ....

Ingredients

Directions :

Day 7

My System 20 Morning Routine

Date: Calories:

Meditation & Stretch

Start time   ....

Duration   ....

Meditation score ....

1	2	3	4	5
V. Poor			V. Good	

Coffee with MCT oil

Start time   ....

Duration   ....

Coffee MCT oil score ....

1	2	3	4	5
V. Poor			V. Good	

Cardio Routine

Start time   ....

Duration   ....

Cardio score   ....

1	2	3	4	5
V. Poor			V. Good	

Notes

....
....
....
....
....
....
....
....
....
....
....

My System 20 Diet Daily Plan

Date: Calories:

No Breakfast

Skip breakfast

Start eating at 11 a.m

Start eating time   ....

Start eating score   ....

1	2	3	4	5
V. Poor				V. Good

Lunch

.... tbsp apple cider vinegar

Beans   ....

Greens   ....

Protiens   ....

Lunch score   ....

1	2	3	4	5
V. Poor				V. Good

Snacks

Lean deli meat	....
Nuts	....
Guacamole	....
Cottage	....
Cheese	....
Green olives	....
Kale Chips	....
Eggs	....
Cheese Chips	....
Snacks score	....

1	2	3	4	5
V. Poor				V. Good

Dinner

.... tbsp apple cider vinegar

Beans   ....

Greens   ....

Protiens   ....

Dinner score   ....

Stop eating at 7 PM

Stop eating score ....

1	2	3	4	5
V. Poor				V. Good

My System 20 Night Routine

Date: _____   Calories: _____

Sleep

Went to bed at ....

Take to fall asleep ....

Get out of bed at ....

Total sleep hours ....

Sleep score ....

1	2	3	4	5
V. Poor			V. Good	

Wake up

Wake up goal at ....

Actual wake up at ....

Wake up score ....

Wake up same
Time score ....

1	2	3	4	5
V. Poor			V. Good	

To do

Turned off tech at ....

Turning off tech score ....

Text conversation with
....

No caffeine at ....

No caffeine score ....

1	2	3	4	5
V. Poor			V. Good	

Notes

....
....
....
....
....
....
....
....
....
....
....

My System 20 Recipe

Prep Time : | Cook Time : | Serves :

Name : ....

Ingredients

....
....
....
....
....
....
....
....
....
....
....

Directions :

....
....
....
....
....
....
....
....

My System 20 Recipe

Prep Time : | Cook Time : | Serves :

Name : ....

Ingredients

....

....

....

....

....

....

....

....

....

....

Directions :

....

....

....

....

....

....

....

....

My System 20 Recipe

Prep Time : | Cook Time : | Serves :

Name : ....

Ingredients

....
....
....
....
....
....
....
....
....
....
....

Directions :

....
....
....
....
....
....
....
....

Day 8

My System 20 Morning Routine

Date: Calories:

Meditation & Stretch

Start time   ....

Duration   ....

Meditation score ....

1	2	3	4	5
V. Poor			V. Good	

Coffee with MCT oil

Start time   ....

Duration   ....

Coffee MCT oil score ....

1	2	3	4	5
V. Poor			V. Good	

Cardio Routine

Start time   ....

Duration   ....

Cardio score   ....

1	2	3	4	5
V. Poor			V. Good	

Notes

....
....
....
....
....
....
....
....
....
....

My System 20 Diet Daily Plan

Date: Calories:

No Breakfast

Skip breakfast

Start eating at 11 a.m

Start eating time ....

Start eating score ....

1	2	3	4	5
V. Poor			V. Good	

Lunch

.... tbsp apple cider vinegar

Beans   ....

Greens   ....

Protiens   ....

Lunch score   ....

1	2	3	4	5
V. Poor			V. Good	

Snacks

Lean deli meat	....
Nuts	....
Guacamole	....
Cottage	....
Cheese	....
Green olives	....
Kale Chips	....
Eggs	....
Cheese Chips	....
Snacks score	....

1	2	3	4	5
V. Poor			V. Good	

Dinner

.... tbsp apple cider vinegar

Beans   ....

Greens   ....

Protiens   ....

Dinner score   ....

Stop eating at 7 PM

Stop eating score ....

1	2	3	4	5
V. Poor			V. Good	

My System 20 Night Routine

Date: Calories:

Sleep

Went to bed at ....

Take to fall asleep ....

Get out of bed at ....

Total sleep hours ....

Sleep score ....

1	2	3	4	5
V. Poor				V. Good

Wake up

Wake up goal at ....

Actual wake up at ....

Wake up score ....

Wake up same
Time score ....

1	2	3	4	5
V. Poor				V. Good

To do

Turned off tech at ....

Turning off tech score ....

Text conversation with
....

No caffeine at ....

No caffeine score ....

1	2	3	4	5
V. Poor				V. Good

Notes

....
....
....
....
....
....
....
....
....

My System 20 Recipe

Prep Time : | Cook Time : | Serves :

Name : ....

Ingredients

Directions :

My System 20 Recipe

Prep Time : | Cook Time : | Serves :

Name : ....

Ingredients

....

....

....

....

....

....

....

....

....

....

Directions :

....

....

....

....

....

....

....

....

My System 20 Recipe

Prep Time : | Cook Time : | Serves :

Name : ....

Ingredients

....

....

....

....

....

....

....

....

....

....

....

Directions :

....

....

....

....

....

....

....

....

....

Day 9

My System 20 Morning Routine

Date: Calories:

Meditation & Stretch

Start time   ....

Duration   ....

Meditation score   ....

1	2	3	4	5
V. Poor			V. Good	

Coffee with MCT oil

Start time   ....

Duration   ....

Coffee MCT oil score   ....

1	2	3	4	5
V. Poor			V. Good	

Cardio Routine

Start time   ....

Duration   ....

Cardio score   ....

1	2	3	4	5
V. Poor			V. Good	

Notes

....
....
....
....
....
....
....
....
....
....

My System 20 Diet Daily Plan

Date: Calories:

No Breakfast

Skip breakfast

Start eating at 11 a.m

Start eating time ....

Start eating score ....

1	2	3	4	5
V. Poor			V. Good	

Lunch

.... tbsp apple cider vinegar

Beans   ....

Greens   ....

Protiens   ....

Lunch score   ....

1	2	3	4	5
V. Poor			V. Good	

Snacks

Lean deli meat   ....

Nuts   ....

Guacamole   ....

Cottage   ....

Cheese

Green olives   ....

Kale Chips   ....

Eggs   ....

Cheese Chips   ....

Snacks score   ....

1	2	3	4	5
V. Poor			V. Good	

Dinner

.... tbsp apple cider vinegar

Beans   ....

Greens   ....

Protiens   ....

Dinner score   ....

Stop eating at 7 PM

Stop eating score ....

1	2	3	4	5
V. Poor			V. Good	

My System 20 Night Routine

Date: _____   Calories: _____

Sleep

Went to bed at ....

Take to fall asleep ....

Get out of bed at ....

Total sleep hours ....

Sleep score ....

1	2	3	4	5
V. Poor			V. Good	

Wake up

Wake up goal at ....

Actual wake up at ....

Wake up score ....

Wake up same
Time score ....

1	2	3	4	5
V. Poor			V. Good	

To do

Turned off tech at ....

Turning off tech score ....

Text conversation with
....

No caffeine at ....

No caffeine score ....

1	2	3	4	5
V. Poor			V. Good	

Notes

....
....
....
....
....
....
....
....
....
....
....

My System 20 Recipe

Prep Time : | Cook Time : | Serves :

Name : ....

Ingredients

....

....

....

....

....

....

....

....

....

....

....

Directions :

....

....

....

....

....

....

....

....

....

My System 20 Recipe

Prep Time : | Cook Time : | Serves :

Name : ....

Ingredients

....
....
....
....
....
....
....
....
....
....
....

Directions :

....
....
....
....
....
....
....
....
....
....

My System 20 Recipe

Prep Time : | Cook Time : | Serves :

Name : ....

Ingredients

....

....

....

....

....

....

....

....

....

....

....

Directions :

....

....

....

....

....

....

....

Day 10

My System 20 Morning Routine

Date: _____   Calories: _____

Meditation & Stretch

Start time   ....

Duration   ....

Meditation score   ....

1	2	3	4	5
V. Poor			V. Good	

Coffee with MCT oil

Start time   ....

Duration   ....

Coffee MCT oil score   ....

1	2	3	4	5
V. Poor			V. Good	

Cardio Routine

Start time   ....

Duration   ....

Cardio score   ....

1	2	3	4	5
V. Poor			V. Good	

Notes

....
....
....
....
....
....
....
....
....
....

My System 20 Diet Daily Plan

Date: Calories:

No Breakfast

Skip breakfast

Start eating at 11 a.m

Start eating time ....

Start eating score ....

1	2	3	4	5
V. Poor			V. Good	

Lunch

.... tbsp apple cider vinegar

Beans ....

Greens ....

Protiens ....

Lunch score ....

1	2	3	4	5
V. Poor			V. Good	

Snacks

Lean deli meat ....

Nuts ....

Guacamole ....

Cottage ....

Cheese ....

Green olives ....

Kale Chips ....

Eggs ....

Cheese Chips ....

Snacks score ....

1	2	3	4	5
V. Poor			V. Good	

Dinner

.... tbsp apple cider vinegar

Beans ....

Greens ....

Protiens ....

Dinner score ....

Stop eating at 7 PM

Stop eating score ....

1	2	3	4	5
V. Poor			V. Good	

My System 20 Night Routine

Date: Calories:

Sleep

Went to bed at ....

Take to fall asleep ....

Get out of bed at ....

Total sleep hours ....

Sleep score ....

1	2	3	4	5
V. Poor			V. Good	

Wake up

Wake up goal at ....

Actual wake up at ....

Wake up score ....

Wake up same
Time score ....

1	2	3	4	5
V. Poor			V. Good	

To do

Turned off tech at ....

Turning off tech score ....

Text conversation with
....

No caffeine at ....

No caffeine score ....

1	2	3	4	5
V. Poor			V. Good	

Notes

....
....
....
....
....
....
....
....
....
....
....

My System 20 Recipe

Prep Time : | Cook Time : | Serves :

Name : ....

Ingredients

....

....

....

....

....

....

....

....

....

....

....

Directions :

....

....

....

....

....

....

....

....

My System 20 Recipe

Prep Time : | Cook Time : | Serves :

Name : ....

Ingredients

....
....
....
....
....
....
....
....
....
....
....

Directions :

....
....
....
....
....
....
....
....
....

My System 20 Recipe

Prep Time : | Cook Time : | Serves :

Name : ....

Ingredients

....
....
....
....
....
....
....
....
....

Directions :

....
....
....
....
....
....
....
....

Day 11

My System 20 Morning Routine

Date: Calories:

Meditation & Stretch

Start time   ....

Duration   ....

Meditation score ....

1	2	3	4	5
V. Poor			V. Good	

Coffee with MCT oil

Start time   ....

Duration   ....

Coffee MCT oil score ....

1	2	3	4	5
V. Poor			V. Good	

Cardio Routine

Start time   ....

Duration   ....

Cardio score   ....

1	2	3	4	5
V. Poor			V. Good	

Notes

....
....
....
....
....
....
....
....
....
....

My System 20 Diet Daily Plan

Date: _____   Calories: _____

No Breakfast

Skip breakfast

Start eating at 11 a.m

Start eating time ....

Start eating score ....

1	2	3	4	5
V. Poor				V. Good

Lunch

.... tbsp apple cider vinegar

Beans   ....

Greens   ....

Protiens   ....

Lunch score   ....

1	2	3	4	5
V. Poor				V. Good

Snacks

Lean deli meat	....
Nuts	....
Guacamole	....
Cottage	....
Cheese	....
Green olives	....
Kale Chips	....
Eggs	....
Cheese Chips	....

Snacks score   ....

1	2	3	4	5
V. Poor				V. Good

Dinner

.... tbsp apple cider vinegar

Beans   ....

Greens   ....

Protiens   ....

Dinner score   ....

Stop eating at 7 PM

Stop eating score ....

1	2	3	4	5
V. Poor				V. Good

My System 20 Night Routine

Date: Calories:

Sleep

Went to bed at ....

Take to fall asleep ....

Get out of bed at ....

Total sleep hours ....

Sleep score ....

1	2	3	4	5
V. Poor			V. Good	

Wake up

Wake up goal at ....

Actual wake up at ....

Wake up score ....

Wake up same
Time score ....

1	2	3	4	5
V. Poor			V. Good	

To do

Turned off tech at ....

Turning off tech score ....

Text conversation with
....

No caffeine at ....

No caffeine score ....

1	2	3	4	5
V. Poor			V. Good	

Notes

....
....
....
....
....
....
....
....
....
....

My System 20 Recipe

Prep Time : | Cook Time : | Serves :

Name : ....

Ingredients

....
....
....
....
....
....
....
....
....
....
....

Directions :

....
....
....
....
....
....
....
....

My System 20 Recipe

Prep Time : | Cook Time : | Serves :

Name : ....

Ingredients

Directions :

My System 20 Recipe

Prep Time :　　　　| Cook Time :　　　　| Serves :

Name : ....

Ingredients

....
....
....
....
....
....
....
....
....
....
....

Directions :

....
....
....
....
....
....
....
....

Day 12

My System 20 Morning Routine

Date: Calories:

Meditation & Stretch

Start time   ....

Duration   ....

Meditation score ....

1	2	3	4	5
V. Poor			V. Good	

Coffee with MCT oil

Start time   ....

Duration   ....

Coffee MCT oil score ....

1	2	3	4	5
V. Poor			V. Good	

Cardio Routine

Start time   ....

Duration   ....

Cardio score   ....

1	2	3	4	5
V. Poor			V. Good	

Notes

....
....
....
....
....
....
....
....
....

My System 20 Diet Daily Plan

Date: Calories:

No Breakfast

Skip breakfast

Start eating at 11 a.m

Start eating time ....

Start eating score ....

1	2	3	4	5
V. Poor			V. Good	

Lunch

.... tbsp apple cider vinegar

Beans   ....

Greens   ....

Protiens   ....

Lunch score   ....

1	2	3	4	5
V. Poor			V. Good	

Snacks

Lean deli meat	....
Nuts	....
Guacamole	....
Cottage	....
Cheese	....
Green olives	....
Kale Chips	....
Eggs	....
Cheese Chips	....
Snacks score	....

1	2	3	4	5
V. Poor			V. Good	

Dinner

.... tbsp apple cider vinegar

Beans   ....

Greens   ....

Protiens   ....

Dinner score   ....

Stop eating at 7 PM

Stop eating score ....

1	2	3	4	5
V. Poor			V. Good	

My System 20 Night Routine

Date: Calories:

Sleep

Went to bed at ....

Take to fall asleep ....

Get out of bed at ....

Total sleep hours ....

Sleep score ....

1	2	3	4	5
V. Poor			V. Good	

Wake up

Wake up goal at ....

Actual wake up at ....

Wake up score ....

Wake up same
Time score ....

1	2	3	4	5
V. Poor			V. Good	

To do

Turned off tech at ....

Turning off tech score ....

Text conversation with
....

No caffeine at ....

No caffeine score ....

1	2	3	4	5
V. Poor			V. Good	

Notes

....
....
....
....
....
....
....
....
....
....

My System 20 Recipe

Prep Time : | Cook Time : | Serves :

Name : ....

Ingredients

Directions :

My System 20 Recipe

Prep Time : | Cook Time : | Serves :

Name : ....

Ingredients

Directions :

My System 20 Recipe

Prep Time : | Cook Time : | Serves :

Name : ....

Ingredients

....
....
....
....
....
....
....
....
....
....

Directions :

....
....
....
....
....
....
....
....

Day 13

My System 20 Morning Routine

Date: Calories:

Meditation & Stretch

Start time   ....

Duration   ....

Meditation score ....

1	2	3	4	5
V. Poor			V. Good	

Coffee with MCT oil

Start time   ....

Duration   ....

Coffee MCT oil score ....

1	2	3	4	5
V. Poor			V. Good	

Cardio Routine

Start time   ....

Duration   ....

Cardio score   ....

1	2	3	4	5
V. Poor			V. Good	

Notes

....
....
....
....
....
....
....
....
....
....
....
....

My System 20 Diet Daily Plan

Date: Calories:

No Breakfast

Skip breakfast

Start eating at 11 a.m

Start eating time ....

Start eating score ....

1	2	3	4	5
V. Poor			V. Good	

Lunch

.... tbsp apple cider vinegar

Beans   ....

Greens   ....

Protiens   ....

Lunch score   ....

1	2	3	4	5
V. Poor			V. Good	

Snacks

Lean deli meat	....
Nuts	....
Guacamole	....
Cottage	....
Cheese	....
Green olives	....
Kale Chips	....
Eggs	....
Cheese Chips	....
Snacks score	....

1	2	3	4	5
V. Poor			V. Good	

Dinner

.... tbsp apple cider vinegar

Beans   ....

Greens   ....

Protiens   ....

Dinner score   ....

Stop eating at 7 PM

Stop eating score ....

1	2	3	4	5
V. Poor			V. Good	

My System 20 Night Routine

Date: Calories:

Sleep

Went to bed at ....

Take to fall asleep ....

Get out of bed at ....

Total sleep hours ....

Sleep score ....

1	2	3	4	5
V. Poor				V. Good

Wake up

Wake up goal at ....

Actual wake up at ....

Wake up score ....

Wake up same
Time score ....

1	2	3	4	5
V. Poor				V. Good

To do

Turned off tech at ....

Turning off tech score ....

Text conversation with
....

No caffeine at ....

No caffeine score ....

1	2	3	4	5
V. Poor				V. Good

Notes

....
....
....
....
....
....
....
....
....

90

My System 20 Recipe

Prep Time : | Cook Time : | Serves :

Name : ....

Ingredients

....
....
....
....
....
....
....
....
....
....
....

Directions :

....
....
....
....
....
....
....
....

My System 20 Recipe

Prep Time : | Cook Time : | Serves :

Name : ....

Ingredients

....
....
....
....
....
....
....
....
....

Directions :

....
....
....
....
....
....
....
....

My System 20 Recipe

Prep Time : | Cook Time : | Serves :

Name : ....

Ingredients

....
....
....
....
....
....
....
....
....
....
....

Directions :

....
....
....
....
....
....
....
....
....
....

Day 14

My System 20 Morning Routine

Date: Calories:

Meditation & Stretch

Start time   ....

Duration   ....

Meditation score   ....

1	2	3	4	5
V. Poor			V. Good	

Coffee with MCT oil

Start time   ....

Duration   ....

Coffee MCT oil score   ....

1	2	3	4	5
V. Poor			V. Good	

Cardio Routine

Start time   ....

Duration   ....

Cardio score   ....

1	2	3	4	5
V. Poor			V. Good	

Notes

....
....
....
....
....
....
....
....
....
....
....

My System 20 Diet Daily Plan

Date: Calories:

No Breakfast

Skip breakfast

Start eating at 11 a.m

Start eating time ....

Start eating score ....

1	2	3	4	5
V. Poor			V. Good	

Lunch

.... tbsp apple cider vinegar

Beans   ....

Greens   ....

Protiens   ....

Lunch score   ....

1	2	3	4	5
V. Poor			V. Good	

Snacks

Lean deli meat   ....
Nuts   ....
Guacamole   ....
Cottage   ....
Cheese   ....
Green olives   ....
Kale Chips   ....
Eggs   ....
Cheese Chips   ....

Snacks score   ....

1	2	3	4	5
V. Poor			V. Good	

Dinner

.... tbsp apple cider vinegar

Beans   ....

Greens   ....

Protiens   ....

Dinner score   ....

Stop eating at 7 PM

Stop eating score ....

1	2	3	4	5
V. Poor			V. Good	

My System 20 Night Routine

Sleep

Went to bed at ....

Take to fall asleep ....

Get out of bed at ....

Total sleep hours ....

Sleep score ....

1	2	3	4	5
V. Poor			V. Good	

Wake up

Wake up goal at ....

Actual wake up at ....

Wake up score ....

Wake up same
Time score ....

1	2	3	4	5
V. Poor			V. Good	

To do

Turned off tech at ....

Turning off tech score ....

Text conversation with
....

No caffeine at ....

No caffeine score ....

1	2	3	4	5
V. Poor			V. Good	

Notes

....
....
....
....
....
....
....
....
....

My System 20 Recipe

Prep Time : | Cook Time : | Serves :

Name : ....

Ingredients

....
....
....
....
....
....
....
....
....
....

Directions :

....
....
....
....
....
....
....
....

My System 20 Recipe

Prep Time : | Cook Time : | Serves :

Name : ....

Ingredients

....
....
....
....
....
....
....
....
....
....

Directions :

....
....
....
....
....
....
....
....

My System 20 Recipe

Prep Time : | Cook Time : | Serves :

Name : ....

Ingredients

Directions :

Day 15

My System 20 Morning Routine

Date: .... Calories: ....

Meditation & Stretch

Start time ....

Duration ....

Meditation score ....

1	2	3	4	5
V. Poor			V. Good	

Coffee with MCT oil

Start time ....

Duration ....

Coffee MCT oil score ....

1	2	3	4	5
V. Poor			V. Good	

Cardio Routine

Start time ....

Duration ....

Cardio score ....

1	2	3	4	5
V. Poor			V. Good	

Notes

....
....
....
....
....
....
....
....
....
....
....
....

My System 20 Diet Daily Plan

Date: Calories:

No Breakfast

Skip breakfast

Start eating at 11 a.m

Start eating time ....

Start eating score ....

1	2	3	4	5
V. Poor			V. Good	

Lunch

.... tbsp apple cider vinegar

Beans ....

Greens ....

Protiens ....

Lunch score ....

1	2	3	4	5
V. Poor			V. Good	

Snacks

Lean deli meat	....
Nuts	....
Guacamole	....
Cottage	....
Cheese	....
Green olives	....
Kale Chips	....
Eggs	....
Cheese Chips	....

Snacks score ....

1	2	3	4	5
V. Poor			V. Good	

Dinner

.... tbsp apple cider vinegar

Beans ....

Greens ....

Protiens ....

Dinner score ....

Stop eating at 7 PM

Stop eating score ....

1	2	3	4	5
V. Poor			V. Good	

My System 20 Night Routine

Date: Calories:

Sleep

Went to bed at ....

Take to fall asleep ....

Get out of bed at ....

Total sleep hours ....

Sleep score   ....

1	2	3	4	5
V. Poor			V. Good	

Wake up

Wake up goal at ....

Actual wake up at ....

Wake up score   ....

Wake up same
Time score   ....

1	2	3	4	5
V. Poor			V. Good	

To do

Turned off tech at ....

Turning off tech score ....

Text conversation with
....

No caffeine at ....

No caffeine score ....

1	2	3	4	5
V. Poor			V. Good	

Notes

....
....
....
....
....
....
....
....
....
....

My System 20 Recipe

Prep Time : | Cook Time : | Serves :

Name : ....

Ingredients

....
....
....
....
....
....
....
....
....
....
....

Directions :

....
....
....
....
....
....
....
....

My System 20 Recipe

Prep Time : | Cook Time : | Serves :

Name : ....

Ingredients

....
....
....
....
....
....
....
....
....
....
....
....

Directions :

....
....
....
....
....
....
....
....
....
....

My System 20 Recipe

Prep Time : | Cook Time : | Serves :

Name : ....

Ingredients

....

....

....

....

....

....

....

....

....

Directions :

....

....

....

....

....

....

....

....

Day 16

My System 20 Morning Routine

Date: Calories:

Meditation & Stretch

Start time   ....

Duration   ....

Meditation score   ....

1	2	3	4	5
V. Poor			V. Good	

Coffee with MCT oil

Start time   ....

Duration   ....

Coffee MCT oil score ....

1	2	3	4	5
V. Poor			V. Good	

Cardio Routine

Start time   ....

Duration   ....

Cardio score   ....

1	2	3	4	5
V. Poor			V. Good	

Notes

....

....

....

....

....

....

....

....

....

....

My System 20 Diet Daily Plan

Date: Calories:

No Breakfast

Skip breakfast

Start eating at 11 a.m

Start eating time ....

Start eating score ....

1	2	3	4	5
V. Poor			V. Good	

Lunch

.... tbsp apple cider vinegar

Beans   ....

Greens   ....

Protiens   ....

Lunch score   ....

1	2	3	4	5
V. Poor			V. Good	

Snacks

Lean deli meat	....
Nuts	....
Guacamole	....
Cottage	....
Cheese	....
Green olives	....
Kale Chips	....
Eggs	....
Cheese Chips	....
Snacks score	....

1	2	3	4	5
V. Poor			V. Good	

Dinner

.... tbsp apple cider vinegar

Beans   ....

Greens   ....

Protiens   ....

Dinner score   ....

Stop eating at 7 PM

Stop eating score ....

1	2	3	4	5
V. Poor			V. Good	

My System 20 Night Routine

Date: Calories:

Sleep

Went to bed at ....

Take to fall asleep ....

Get out of bed at ....

Total sleep hours ....

Sleep score   ....

1	2	3	4	5
V. Poor			V. Good	

Wake up

Wake up goal at ....

Actual wake up at ....

Wake up score ....

Wake up same
Time score   ....

1	2	3	4	5
V. Poor			V. Good	

To do

Turned off tech at ....

Turning off tech score ....

Text conversation with

....

No caffeine at ....

No caffeine score ....

1	2	3	4	5
V. Poor			V. Good	

Notes

....

....

....

....

....

....

....

....

....

....

....

My System 20 Recipe

Prep Time : | Cook Time : | Serves :

Name : ....

Ingredients

....

....

....

....

....

....

....

....

....

....

Directions :

....

....

....

....

....

....

....

....

My System 20 Recipe

Prep Time : | Cook Time : | Serves :

Name : ....

Ingredients

....
....
....
....
....
....
....
....
....
....
....

Directions :

....
....
....
....
....
....
....
....

My System 20 Recipe

Prep Time : | Cook Time : | Serves :

Name : ....

Ingredients

....

....

....

....

....

....

....

....

....

....

Directions :

....

....

....

....

....

....

....

....

Day 17

My System 20 Morning Routine

Date: Calories:

Meditation & Stretch

Start time   ....

Duration   ....

Meditation score ....

1	2	3	4	5
V. Poor			V. Good	

Coffee with MCT oil

Start time   ....

Duration   ....

Coffee MCT oil score ....

1	2	3	4	5
V. Poor			V. Good	

Cardio Routine

Start time   ....

Duration   ....

Cardio score   ....

1	2	3	4	5
V. Poor			V. Good	

Notes

....
....
....
....
....
....
....
....
....
....
....

My System 20 Diet Daily Plan

Date: Calories:

No Breakfast

Skip breakfast

Start eating at 11 a.m

Start eating time ....

Start eating score ....

1	2	3	4	5
V. Poor			V. Good	

Lunch

.... tbsp apple cider vinegar

Beans ....

Greens ....

Protiens ....

Lunch score ....

1	2	3	4	5
V. Poor			V. Good	

Snacks

Lean deli meat ....

Nuts ....

Guacamole ....

Cottage ....

Cheese ....

Green olives ....

Kale Chips ....

Eggs ....

Cheese Chips ....

Snacks score ....

1	2	3	4	5
V. Poor			V. Good	

Dinner

.... tbsp apple cider vinegar

Beans ....

Greens ....

Protiens ....

Dinner score ....

Stop eating at 7 PM

Stop eating score ....

1	2	3	4	5
V. Poor			V. Good	

My System 20 Night Routine

Date: Calories:

Sleep

Went to bed at ....

Take to fall asleep ....

Get out of bed at ....

Total sleep hours ....

Sleep score ....

1	2	3	4	5
V. Poor			V. Good	

Wake up

Wake up goal at ....

Actual wake up at ....

Wake up score ....

Wake up same
Time score ....

1	2	3	4	5
V. Poor			V. Good	

To do

Turned off tech at ....

Turning off tech score ....

Text conversation with
....

No caffeine at ....

No caffeine score ....

1	2	3	4	5
V. Poor			V. Good	

Notes

....
....
....
....
....
....
....
....
....
....

My System 20 Recipe

Prep Time : | Cook Time : | Serves :

Name : ....

Ingredients

Directions :

My System 20 Recipe

Prep Time : | Cook Time : | Serves :

Name : ....

Ingredients

Directions :

My System 20 Recipe

Prep Time : | Cook Time : | Serves :

Name : ....

Ingredients

....

....

....

....

....

....

....

....

....

....

....

Directions :

....

....

....

....

....

....

....

....

Day 18

My System 20 Morning Routine

Date: Calories:

Meditation & Stretch

Start time ....

Duration ....

Meditation score ....

1	2	3	4	5
V. Poor			V. Good	

Coffee with MCT oil

Start time ....

Duration ....

Coffee MCT oil score ....

1	2	3	4	5
V. Poor			V. Good	

Cardio Routine

Start time ....

Duration ....

Cardio score ....

1	2	3	4	5
V. Poor			V. Good	

Notes

....
....
....
....
....
....
....
....
....
....
....

My System 20 Diet Daily Plan

Date: Calories:

No Breakfast

Skip breakfast

Start eating at 11 a.m

Start eating time   ....

Start eating score   ....

1	2	3	4	5
V. Poor			V. Good	

Lunch

.... tbsp apple cider vinegar

Beans   ....

Greens   ....

Protiens   ....

Lunch score   ....

1	2	3	4	5
V. Poor			V. Good	

Snacks

Lean deli meat   ....
Nuts   ....
Guacamole   ....
Cottage   ....
Cheese   ....
Green olives   ....
Kale Chips   ....
Eggs   ....
Cheese Chips   ....

Snacks score   ....

1	2	3	4	5
V. Poor			V. Good	

Dinner

.... tbsp apple cider vinegar

Beans   ....

Greens   ....

Protiens   ....

Dinner score   ....

Stop eating at 7 PM

Stop eating score ....

1	2	3	4	5
V. Poor			V. Good	

My System 20 Night Routine

Date: Calories:

Sleep

Went to bed at ....

Take to fall asleep ....

Get out of bed at ....

Total sleep hours ....

Sleep score   ....

1	2	3	4	5
V. Poor			V. Good	

Wake up

Wake up goal at   ....

Actual wake up at   ....

Wake up score   ....

Wake up same
Time score   ....

1	2	3	4	5
V. Poor			V. Good	

To do

Turned off tech at ....

Turning off tech score ....

Text conversation with
....

No caffeine at ....

No caffeine score ....

1	2	3	4	5
V. Poor			V. Good	

Notes

....
....
....
....
....
....
....
....
....
....

My System 20 Recipe

Prep Time : | Cook Time : | Serves :

Name : ....

Ingredients

....

....

....

....

....

....

....

....

....

....

Directions :

....

....

....

....

....

....

....

....

My System 20 Recipe

Prep Time : | Cook Time : | Serves :

Name : ....

Ingredients

....

....

....

....

....

....

....

....

....

....

....

Directions :

....

....

....

....

....

....

....

....

My System 20 Recipe

Prep Time : | Cook Time : | Serves :

Name : ....

Ingredients

....

....

....

....

....

....

....

....

....

....

Directions :

....

....

....

....

....

....

....

....

....

Day 19

My System 20 Morning Routine

Date: Calories:

Meditation & Stretch

Start time   ....

Duration   ....

Meditation score ....

1	2	3	4	5
V. Poor			V. Good	

Coffee with MCT oil

Start time   ....

Duration   ....

Coffee MCT oil score ....

1	2	3	4	5
V. Poor			V. Good	

Cardio Routine

Start time   ....

Duration   ....

Cardio score   ....

1	2	3	4	5
V. Poor			V. Good	

Notes

....
....
....
....
....
....
....
....
....
....

My System 20 Diet Daily Plan

Date: Calories:

No Breakfast

Skip breakfast

Start eating at 11 a.m

Start eating time ....

Start eating score ....

1	2	3	4	5
V. Poor			V. Good	

Lunch

.... tbsp apple cider vinegar

Beans   ....

Greens   ....

Protiens   ....

Lunch score   ....

1	2	3	4	5
V. Poor			V. Good	

Snacks

Lean deli meat	....
Nuts	....
Guacamole	....
Cottage	....
Cheese	....
Green olives	....
Kale Chips	....
Eggs	....
Cheese Chips	....
Snacks score	....

1	2	3	4	5
V. Poor			V. Good	

Dinner

.... tbsp apple cider vinegar

Beans   ....

Greens   ....

Protiens   ....

Dinner score   ....

Stop eating at 7 PM

Stop eating score ....

1	2	3	4	5
V. Poor			V. Good	

My System 20 Night Routine

Date: Calories:

Sleep

Went to bed at ....

Take to fall asleep ....

Get out of bed at ....

Total sleep hours ....

Sleep score   ....

1	2	3	4	5
V. Poor			V. Good	

Wake up

Wake up goal at ....

Actual wake up at ....

Wake up score   ....

Wake up same
Time score   ....

1	2	3	4	5
V. Poor			V. Good	

To do

Turned off tech at ....

Turning off tech score ....

Text conversation with

....

No caffeine at ....

No caffeine score ....

1	2	3	4	5
V. Poor			V. Good	

Notes

....
....
....
....
....
....
....
....
....
....
....

My System 20 Recipe

Prep Time : | Cook Time : | Serves :

Name : ....

Ingredients

....
....
....
....
....
....
....
....
....
....
....

Directions :

....
....
....
....
....
....
....
....
....

My System 20 Recipe

Prep Time :　　　| Cook Time :　　　| Serves :

Name : ....

Ingredients

....
....
....
....
....
....
....
....
....
....

Directions :

....
....
....
....
....
....
....
....
....

My System 20 Recipe

Prep Time : | Cook Time : | Serves :

Name : ....

Ingredients

....
....
....
....
....
....
....
....
....
....
....

Directions :

....
....
....
....
....
....
....
....
....

Day 20

My System 20 Morning Routine

Date: Calories:

Meditation & Stretch

Start time   ....

Duration   ....

Meditation score ....

1	2	3	4	5
V. Poor			V. Good	

Coffee with MCT oil

Start time   ....

Duration   ....

Coffee MCT oil score ....

1	2	3	4	5
V. Poor			V. Good	

Cardio Routine

Start time   ....

Duration   ....

Cardio score   ....

1	2	3	4	5
V. Poor			V. Good	

Notes

....
....
....
....
....
....
....
....
....
....
....

My System 20 Diet Daily Plan

Date: Calories:

No Breakfast

Skip breakfast

Start eating at 11 a.m

Start eating time ....

Start eating score ....

1	2	3	4	5
V. Poor			V. Good	

Lunch

.... tbsp apple cider vinegar

Beans ....

Greens ....

Protiens ....

Lunch score ....

1	2	3	4	5
V. Poor			V. Good	

Snacks

Lean deli meat	....
Nuts	....
Guacamole	....
Cottage	....
Cheese	....
Green olives	....
Kale Chips	....
Eggs	....
Cheese Chips	....
Snacks score	....

1	2	3	4	5
V. Poor			V. Good	

Dinner

.... tbsp apple cider vinegar

Beans ....

Greens ....

Protiens ....

Dinner score ....

Stop eating at 7 PM

Stop eating score ....

1	2	3	4	5
V. Poor			V. Good	

My System 20 Night Routine

Date: Calories:

Sleep

Went to bed at ....

Take to fall asleep ....

Get out of bed at ....

Total sleep hours ....

Sleep score   ....

1	2	3	4	5
V. Poor			V. Good	

Wake up

Wake up goal at   ....

Actual wake up at   ....

Wake up score   ....

Wake up same
Time score   ....

1	2	3	4	5
V. Poor			V. Good	

To do

Turned off tech at ....

Turning off tech score ....

Text conversation with

....

No caffeine at ....

No caffeine score ....

1	2	3	4	5
V. Poor			V. Good	

Notes

....
....
....
....
....
....
....
....
....
....

My System 20 Recipe

Prep Time : | Cook Time : | Serves :

Name : ....

Ingredients

....
....
....
....
....
....
....
....
....
....

Directions :

....
....
....
....
....
....
....
....
....

My System 20 Recipe

Prep Time : | Cook Time : | Serves :

Name : ....

Ingredients

Directions :

Day 20-End

My System 20 Weight Tracker

Date	Weight	Result	Total Lost
Date	Weight	Result	Total Lost

My System 20 Measurements Tracker

Date	Neck	Bust	Arms	Waist	Hips	Thighs
Goal	Neck	Bust	Arms	Waist	Hips	Thighs

My System 20 Notes :

My System 20 Notes :

My System 20 Notes :

My System 20 Notes :

Its 20 days, not 20 years.

Made in the USA
Middletown, DE
26 May 2020